BIOGRAPHIES

SOJOURNER TRUTH

by A.M. Reynolds

PEBBLE
a capstone imprint

Pebble Explore is published by Pebble, an imprint of Capstone.
1710 Roe Crest Drive
North Mankato, Minnesota 56003
www.capstonepub.com

Library of Congress Cataloging-in-Publication Data is available on the Library of Congress website.
ISBN 978-1-9771-2334-3 (library binding)
ISBN 978-1-9771-2659-7 (paperback)
ISBN 978-1-9771-2342-8 (ebook pdf)

Summary: How much do you know about Sojourner Truth? Find out the facts you need to know about this anti-slavery and women's rights activist. You'll learn about the early life, challenges, and major accomplishments of this important American.

Image Credits
Alamy: Alpha Historica, cover, 1; Getty Images: Bettmann, 16, Buyenlarge, 24, Gado/Smith Collection, 12, MPI, 17, The Washington Post/Katherine Frey, 27; Granger: 13, Sarin Images, 8; Library of Congress: 5, 21, 25, 29; The New York Public Library: 14; Newscom: Glasshouse Images, 19; North Wind Picture Archives: 7, 11, 22; Shutterstock: Everett Historical, 20, kapooklook01 (geometric background), cover, back cover, 2, 29, spatuletail, 26

Editorial Credits
Editor: Anna Butzer; Designer: Elyse White; Media Researcher: Svetlana Zhurkin; Production Specialist: Spencer Rosio

All internet sites appearing in back matter were available and accurate when this book was sent to press.

Printed in the United States 6668

Table of Contents

Words in **bold** are in the glossary.

Who Was Sojourner Truth?

Sojourner Truth was brave. She fought to end **slavery**. In the 1800s, many black people in the United States were held against their will by people who **enslaved** them. The enslavers made them work.

Truth could not read or write, but she became famous. She spoke to big groups of people. She told people what life was like being enslaved. This helped them understand slavery was bad. Truth kept fighting even when it was hard. She is an American hero.

Sojourner Truth in 1864

Growing Up Sojourner

Truth was born more than 200 years ago. She was born into slavery. It is believed she was born in 1797.

Her birth name was Isabella Baumfree. Her family members were all enslaved. They lived and were made to work on a farm in Swartekill, New York. She grew up speaking Dutch.

Enslaved people harvested wheat in New York state in the early 1800s.

Truth had at least 10 brothers and sisters. She did not know them all. Her enslaver sold off her brothers and sisters.

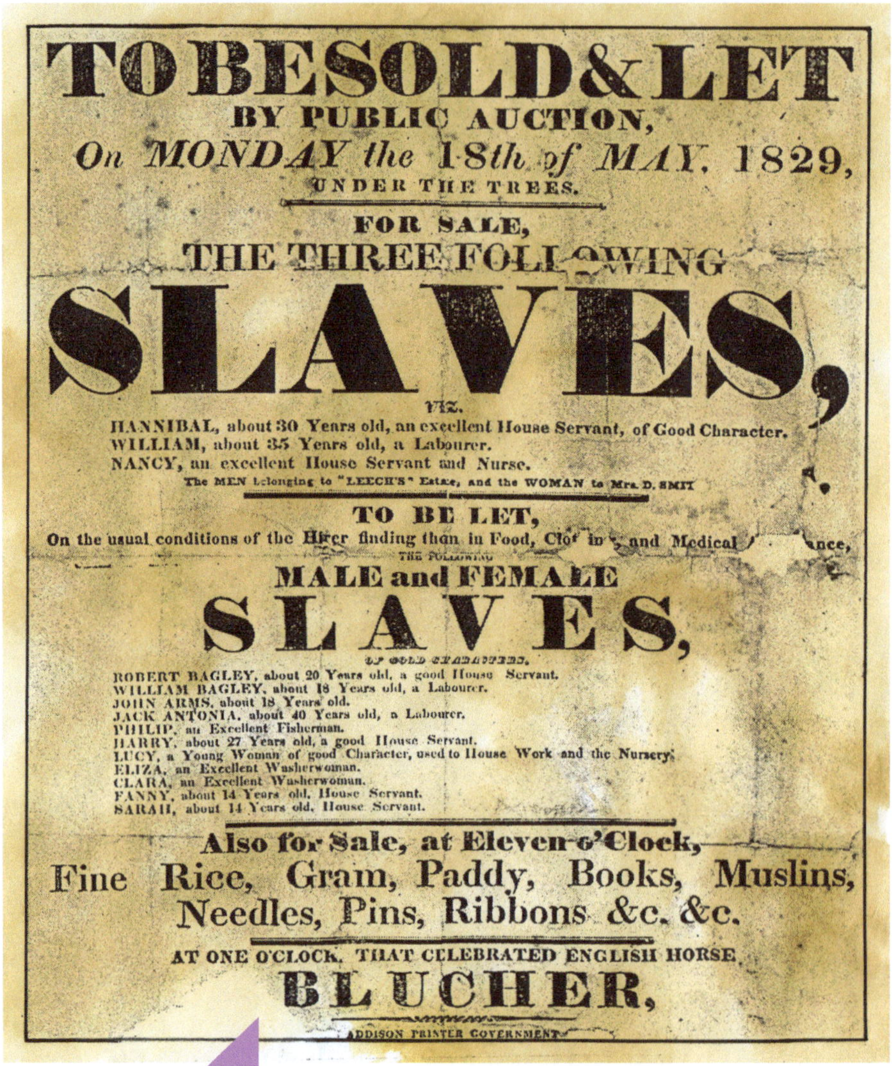

Owners offered enslaved people for sale along with animals, food, and other goods.

When she was 9 years old, Truth was sold. Her new enslaver treated her badly. He beat her for not **obeying** him. Truth could not speak English. She did not understand what he was saying.

Truth was sold two more times. John Dumont bought her. He lived on a farm in West Park, New York. Truth learned to speak English there.

Family

Truth met a man named Robert on a farm nearby. He was also enslaved. She wanted to marry him. Her enslaver would not let her. In 1817, John Dumont made her marry a man he enslaved named Thomas.

Thomas and Truth had four children. All of the children were enslaved too. Truth was scared Dumont would sell her children to someone else. She was scared she would never see her children again.

Children of enslaved people were born into slavery.

John Dumont promised Truth that he would free her. She would no longer be enslaved. Then he changed his mind.

Truth was very upset. She ran away with her youngest daughter. Truth stayed with some neighbors. They thought slavery was wrong. Dumont tried to get Truth back. But the neighbors bought her for $20. Then they freed her.

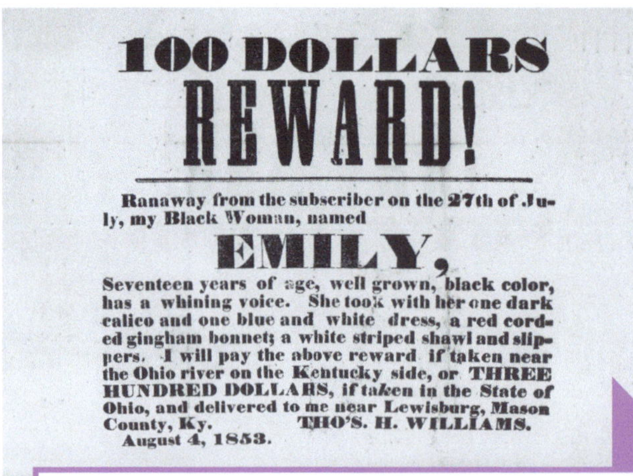

100 DOLLARS

REWARD!

Ranaway from the subscriber on the 27th of July, my Black Woman, named

EMILY,

Seventeen years of age, well grown, black color, has a whining voice. She took with her one dark calico and one blue and white dress, a red corded gingham bonnet; a white striped shawl and slippers. I will pay the above reward if taken near the Ohio river on the Kentucky side, or THREE HUNDRED DOLLARS, if taken in the State of Ohio, and delivered to me near Lewisburg, Mason County, Ky. THO'S. H. WILLIAMS.

August 4, 1853.

Newspaper ads promised rewards for the return of enslaved people who had run away.

A fugitive from slavery with a small bundle of her things

Once separated, many family members would never see each other again.

Dumont sold Truth's 5-year-old son, Peter. He sold him to people in Alabama. In 1827, it was **illegal** to sell a slave to somebody in another state.

Truth went to **court** to fight for her son. She won the court case. She won her son's freedom.

Fighting for Freedom

In 1828, Truth moved to New York City. She worked as a housekeeper. She was paid for her work. She then changed her name to Sojourner Truth.

A New York City street in the 1830s

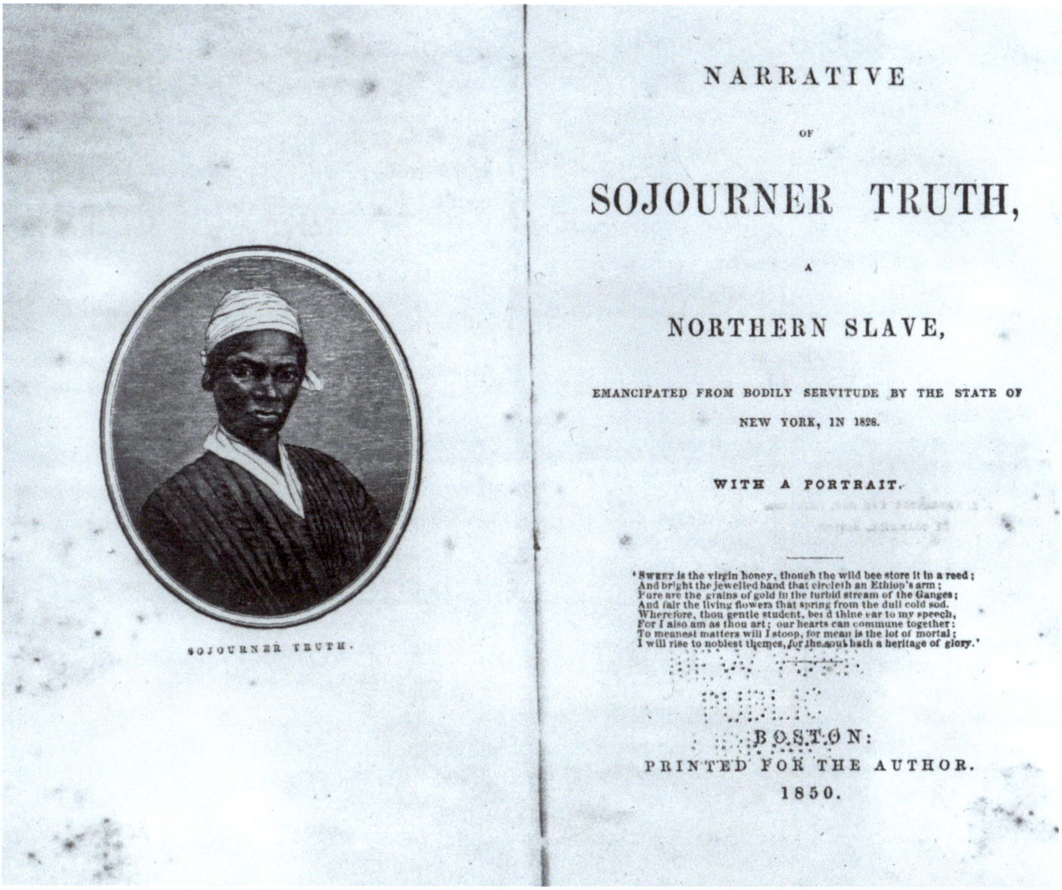

SOJOURNER TRUTH.

NARRATIVE

OF

SOJOURNER TRUTH,

A

NORTHERN SLAVE,

EMANCIPATED FROM BODILY SERVITUDE BY THE STATE OF NEW YORK, IN 1828.

WITH A PORTRAIT.

'Sweet is the virgin honey, though the wild bee store it in a reed;
And bright the jewelled band that circleth an Ethiop's arm;
Pure are the grains of gold in the turbid stream of the Ganges;
And fair the living flowers that spring from the dull cold sod.
Wherefore, thou gentle student, bend thine ear to my speech,
For I also am as thou art; our hearts can commune together:
To meanest matters will I stoop, for mean is the lot of mortal;
I will rise to noblest themes, for the soul hath a heritage of glory.'

BOSTON:
PRINTED FOR THE AUTHOR.
1850.

Truth wanted to share her story, but she still could not read or write. She told her story to a friend. The friend wrote Sojourner's **autobiography** for her.

Truth believed everybody should be free. She thought women should have the same **rights** as men. Women could not vote or have certain jobs. She thought this was wrong.

Truth traveled across America. She became a famous speaker. She spoke about her life when she was enslaved. Her stories helped people to see how terrible slavery was. She wanted it stopped. People listened to her. She was an important leader in the fight to end slavery.

Sojourner Truth told her life story to groups of people.

During the American **Civil War** (1861–1865), many enslaved people became free. Truth helped them find jobs. She told black soldiers to join the **Union** Army. Her own grandson joined. She raised money for army supplies.

Black Union soldiers in 1864

Sojourner met president Abraham Lincoln in 1864.

In 1864, she was invited to Washington, D.C., by the president of the United States, Abraham Lincoln. He wanted to meet her. He listened to her stories of being enslaved. He wanted to make slavery illegal.

People rode in streetcars and carriages in Washington, D.C.

In Washington, D.C., Truth noticed only white people rode in streetcars. She did not think that was fair.

She decided to try to ride in a streetcar. The driver said he would not drive. He tried to keep her off, but Sojourner would not leave. The driver was forced to give her a ride. People heard about her riding in the streetcar. Her brave act made others want to fight for equal rights.

Later Life

After the Civil War, Truth moved to Battle Creek, Michigan. Many enslaved people who had become free lived there. They had little or no money. Truth asked the government to give them land to farm. But she was unsuccessful.

Battle Creek, Michigan, in 1869

Truth grew old, but she still gave speeches. She wanted women to have the right to vote. She kept fighting for equal rights for all people.

Remembering Sojourner

Truth died on November 26, 1883. She was about 86 years old. People remember her today. There are roads and schools named after her. Her picture was on a U.S. postage stamp.

A bronze statue of Sojourner Truth is in the U.S. Capitol.

A statue of her is in the U.S. Capitol. She was the first African American woman to receive this honor. Truth is remembered as a hero who never gave up on what she believed was right.

Important Dates

around 1797	Sojourner Truth is born as Isabella Baumfree in New York. She is enslaved.
1810	John Dumont buys Sojourner.
1826	Dumont promises to free Truth, but he changes his mind. She runs away.
1828	Truth is one of the first African American women to take a white man to court. She wins her case.
1829	Truth moves to New York City.
1843	Truth changes her name from Isabella Baumfree to Sojourner Truth.
1850	Her autobiography is published. She travels to speak against slavery.
1864	Truth visits Washington, D.C. She meets Abraham Lincoln.
1883	Truth dies at her home in Battle Creek, Michigan on November 26.

Fast Facts

Name:
Sojourner Truth
(born as Isabella Baumfree)

Role:
anti-slavery and women's rights activist

Life dates:
around 1797 to November 26, 1883

Key accomplishments:
Sojourner Truth fought against slavery. She gave talks about being enslaved. This helped people realize that slavery was cruel and unfair. She also fought for women's rights. She wanted everybody to have equal rights. She never gave up.

Glossary

autobiography (aw-tuh-by-AH-gruh-fee)—a story based on the writer's own life

civil war (SIV-il WOR)—a war between different sections or parties of the same country or nation

court (KORT)—a place where laws are carried out

enslave (en-SLAYV)—to make someone lose their freedom

illegal (ill-LEE-guhl)—against the law

obey (oh-BAY)—to do what someone tells you to do

right (RYT)—something that everyone should be able to do or to have and that the government shouldn't be able to take away, such as the right to speak freely

slavery (SLAY-vur-ee)—the practice of owning other people; enslaved people are made to work without pay

Union (YOON-yuhn)—the northern states that fought against the Southern states in the American Civil War